Bible Quizzes & Puzzles

TEST YOUR BIBLE KNOWLEDGE

Publications International, Ltd.

Contributing Writers:
June Eaton
Cecil Murphey
Carol Smith
Jeffery Scott Wallace
Linda M. Washington

Louis Weber, CEO
Publications International, Ltd.
7373 North Cicero Avenue
Lincolnwood, Illinois 60712

Permission is never granted for commercial purposes.

ISBN-13: 978-0-7853-9318-4
ISBN-10: 0-7853-9318-8

Manufactured in USA

8 7 6 5 4 3 2 1

CONTENTS

TEST YOUR BIBLE KNOWLEDGE!

The Bible has been a source of inspiration, encouragement, and guidance for countless generations. Perhaps people have enjoyed games and puzzles for just as long a time. With *Bible Quizzes & Puzzles,* adults can have the best of both: As you test your Bible knowledge, the words and the insights of the Bible will inspire and guide you with their profound wisdom.

This book covers the Old and New Testaments from Genesis to Revelation. You will recall once again the great heroes and villains from biblical history, as well as the fascinating kings and queens who ruled Israel and its neighbors. You will ponder key places in the holy land and the historic events that shaped the nation of Israel and the early church. Some questions and puzzles will be easy; others will be challenging. But all will be intriguing.

A wide variety of puzzles and quizzes are included, such as crossword puzzles, crisscross puzzles, cryptograms, unscramble and match puzzles, quotation puzzles, hidden words, and unscramble and solve puzzles. The questions come in many forms as well—identify questions, true or false quizzes, matching, fill in the blanks, and multiple choice. Each chapter contains an assortment of these puzzles and questions, so you'll never be bored.

It's time to begin. So test your Bible knowledge, learn new facts, and, most of all, have fun!

CHAPTER ONE

∾∾∾ **Kings, Queens, and Prophets** ∾∾∾

1. Quotation Puzzle: That's the Question!

To find the verse, put the letters that appear in the bottom half of the puzzle in the column of boxes above them. The letters may not be listed in the exact order in which they appear in the quote. Mark off used letters at the bottom. A letter may be used only once. The black boxes represent the space between words.

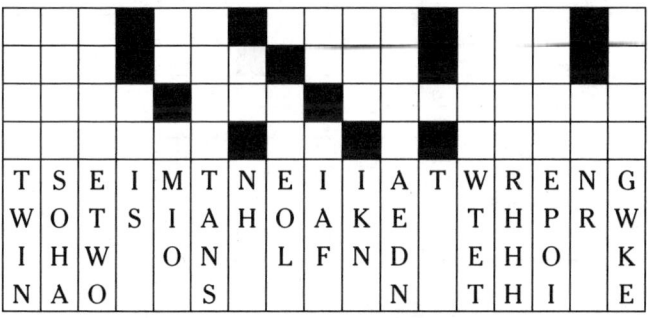

2. True or False: David's best friend was the son of his enemy, King Saul.

3. This king forced his son to pass through fire: (a) Solomon; (b) Jehoshaphat; (c) Hezekiah; (d) Manasseh.

4. Matching

Match the people in Queen Esther's life with the event.

1. Hegai	A. Informed her of the edict
2. Mordecai	B. Chose her to be queen
3. Vashti	C. Plotted against the Jews
4. Haman	D. Took custody of her
5. Ahaseurus	E. Refused to appear

5. Crisscross Puzzle: Kings, Prophets, and Other Men

Answers on page 72.

Fit each of the following 66 words into the puzzle below. Words are arranged below alphabetically according to the number of letters.

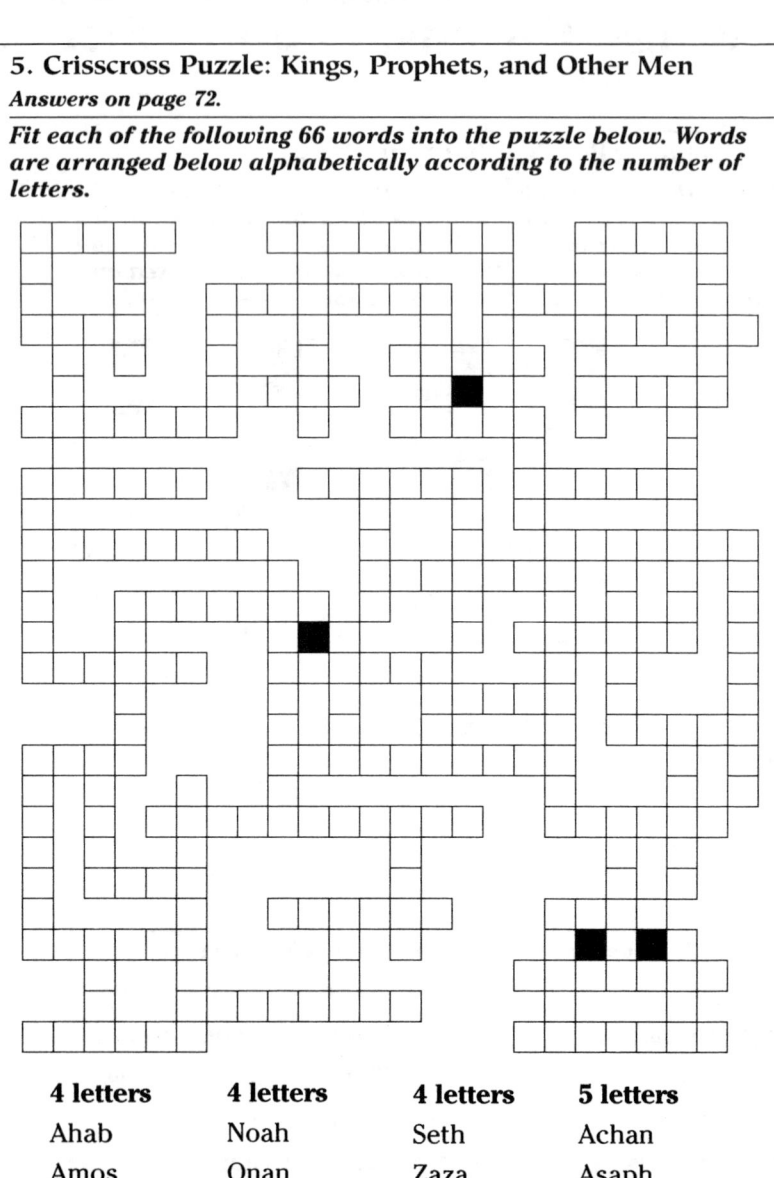

4 letters	4 letters	4 letters	5 letters
Ahab	Noah	Seth	Achan
Amos	Onan	Zaza	Asaph
John	Paul	Zuar	Darda
Luke	Saul		Demas

Crisscross Puzzle *continued*

5 letters	6 letters	6 letters	8 Letters
Elder	Carpus	Uzziah	Abiathar
Hegai	Daniel	**7 letters**	Hezekiah
Hosea	Elisha	Ahaziah	Jeremiah
Isaac	Gideon	Ananias	Onesimus
Jesus	Hezron	Apostle	**9 letters**
Jonah	Hoshea	Bedeiah	Elimelech
Laban	Joseph	Eleazar	Nethaniah
Micah	Josiah	Husband	Zechariah
Moses	Nathan	Malchus	Zephaniah
Peter	Philip	Obadiah	**10 letters**
Uriah	Pilate	Prophet	Ishbosheth
Uriel	Samson	Stephen	Zelophehad
6 letters	Samuel	Timaeus	**11 letters**
Ahiram	Thomas	Zebulun	Melchizedek
Bariah			

6. What son of King David died when he was hung by his hair on a tree?

7. Which prophet had a wife who had "children of whoredom"?

8. True or False: Solomon was the son of King David and Queen Jezebel.

9. What giant did King David kill when he was a young shepherd?

10. True or False: Queen Athaliah, daughter of King Ahab, killed her sons so they wouldn't succeed her to the throne.

11. Unscramble and Match: Plants and Animals

Unscramble the names of the plants and animals on the left, and match them with the king, prophet, or other person associated with each one.

1. CASYROEM REET (Luke 19:4) _____ BALAAM

2. NILO (Dan 6:16–24) _____ SAMSON

3. LAQUI (Num 11:31) _____ DANIEL

4. LIVEO ELFA (Gen 8:11) _____ ZACCHAEUS

5. KOCC (Mark 13:35) _____ MOSES

6. EBSE (Judg 14:8) _____ JEWISH EXILES

7. PHEES (1 Sam 17:15) _____ PETER

8. KENDOY (Num 22:28–30) _____ DAVID

9. LOWWIL REET (Psa 137:2) _____ SOLOMON

10. DARCE REETS (1 Ki 5:6) _____ NOAH

---

12. True or False: Anna was the prophetess at the temple who recognized the infant Jesus as the Messiah.

13. Fill in the blank: "_____ was eight years old when he began to reign; he reigned thirty-one years in Jerusalem" (2 Ki 22:1).

14. Who was Boaz and Ruth's royal great-grandson?

15. True or False: The Prophet Isaiah was the son of King Solomon.

16. Fill in the blank: King David said to the whole assembly, "My son _____, whom alone God has chosen, is young and inexperienced, and the work is great; for the temple will not be for mortals but for the Lord God" (1 Chron 29:1).

---

17. Hidden Words: Bible Types

Among the contents of the Bible are the following types of writing. Find these words hidden in the sentences below.

law	history	prophecy	prayer	poetry
hymn	gospel	letters	sermon	parable

1. "Be sure to bring your #2 pencils and an eraser Monday for the test," announced the teacher.

2. Don't try to enlist in the Marines if your health is below par. Able-bodied recruits are the only ones being accepted.

3. My cousin Lila works in a doctor's office.

4. The Whigs opposed the British king and his Tory sympathizers.

5. A good author for mystery lovers is Edgar Allan Poe. Try reading some of his macabre short stories.

6. "Cheer up, Ray; Eric has volunteered to work your shift tonight."

7. "Let terse, angry words be put aside in the interest of peace," the ambassador pleaded.

8. The Galapagos, Pelau, and Canary Islands are among the places I hope to visit.

9. Unless you approach them with complete apathy, mnemonic techniques really can assist your memory.

10. When asked to design a stage prop, he cycled back to the office and got right to work.

18. Crossword Puzzle: Bible Details *Answers on page 78.*

*(*Denotes name of Bible book)*

Across

*1 A priest after the exile

*7 Fourth Gospel

11 Gather crops (Lev 19:9)

13 Geber was _____'_ son (1 Ki 4:19)

14 17th letter of the Greek alphabet

15 Cave or lair (Nah 2:11)

17 A record of events in the Bible

21 Babylonian god of wisdom

*23 Prophet concerned with social evils

24 Copper coin of ancient Rome

25 Speak to God (Job 33:26)

27 Rave (Prov 29:9)

29 Aid (Ex 18:4)

*33 Devoted daughter-in-law

34 God's Word (2 wds)

37 Philistine seaport (Gen 10:19)

38 A city of Judah (Josh 15:15)

39 One who colors a garment (Job 38:14)

42 Associate with (Psa 26:4)

48 Asian city visited by Paul (Acts 18:19)

53 Sacred writings (2 wds)
(Acts 18:24)

56 He rebuked Job's friends
(Job 32:2)

60 Pair (Gen 6:19)

61 Lord (Hebrew)

*65 Prophet with an unfaith-
ful wife

*66 Prophet who called
Nineveh to repent

Down

1 Judah's son (Gen 38:3)

2 Fortified town (Josh 19:35)

3 Cheer

4 "Hidden" books of the
Bible

5 Violent weather
(Acts 27:18)

6 Lit stick (Gen 15:17)

*7 Bible letter writer; sinned
(2 wds)

8 Metal-bearing rock
(Job 28:2)

9 Hebrew measure
(Ex 30:24)

10 Opposite directions
(abbr)

12 Metallic element

16 A son of David
(2 Sam 5:15)

18 Liquid from olives
(Ex 27:20)

19 God's name (Ex 3:14)

*20 Jewish queen of Persia

22 Plural of is

24 A model worker
(Prov 6:6)

26 Aluminum (symbol)

28 Gold (symbol)

30 Noah was 500 years _____.
(Gen 5:32)

31 Aramaic for "father"
(Mark 14:36)

32 Snake without vowels

35 Ancient form of "you"

36 Roman two

*40 He led invasion of
Canaan

41 "Though only ____ _____
being..." (John 10:33).
(2 wds)

43 Old Testament (abbr)

44 New Hampshire (abbr)

45 Southeast (abbr)

46 Roman Catholic (abbr)

47 "Speaking the _____ in
love" (Eph 4:15).

48 Priestly garment
(Ex 28:4)

49 Platinum (symbol)

50 Hesitation in speech

51 Selenium (abbr)

52 Self and another

*54 He rebuilt Jerusalem's
walls (abbr)

*55 Friend to Paul (abbr)
(Acts 16:1)

57 Behold (Isa 17:14)

58 "It _____ written"
(Mark 1:2).

59 "_____ is the Son of God"
(Acts 9:20).

62 District Attorney (abbr)

63 Expression of surprise

64 13th letter of Greek alphabet

---

19. Matching

Match the king with his nation.

1. Darius	A. Israel
2. Jeroboam	B. Babylon
3. Nebuchadnezzar	C. Assyria
4. Hezekiah	D. Media
5. Sennacherib	E. Judah

---

20. Who made King Herod aware of the birth of the Messiah? (a) chief priests; (b) scribes; (c) wise men; (d) John the Baptist.

21. Who was the Jewish orphan girl who later became queen of Persia?

22. This man became a wicked king of Judah at the age of 12: (a) Josiah; (b) Manasseh; (c) Joash; (d) Uzziah.

23. What was Jeremiah's response when God called him to prophesy? (a) I am just a child; (b) I am just a man; (c) I don't speak well; (d) I have to bury my father.

---

24. Cryptogram: A King of God's Choosing

Decode the letters in the words of this Bible verse. Each letter corresponds to a different letter in the alphabet.

VCJ PZFS CHQ QZXTCV ZXV H DHK HNVJF CUQ ZRK CJHFV; HKS VCJ PZFS CHQ HEEZUKVJS CUD VZ AJ FXPJF ZGJF CUQ EJZEPJ.

---

25. Unscramble and Solve: Elijah and the Birds

Rearrange the letters after each number to form a word. Then rearrange the boxed letters to form the answer to the statement. The answer is a play on words.

How Elijah felt in the wilderness before God sent some birds to feed him:

He was "__ __ __ __ __-__ __ __."

1. DEFE __ ☐ __ __

2. KRIND __ __ __ ☐ __

3. BADER __ ☐ __ __ __ __

4. TEAM __ __ ☐ __

5. DEVIL __ __ ☐ __ __

6. ORWD __ ☐ __ __

7. SATE __ __ __ ☐

8. RUNT __ ☐ __ __

---

26. Fill in the blanks: The lover in the Song of Solomon declared, "I am a _____ of Sharon, a _____ of the valleys" (Sol 2:1).

27. Fill in the blank: Isaiah declared, "He will not cry or lift up his voice . . . a bruised _____ he will not break" (Isa 42:2–3).

28. Fill in the blanks: Isaiah proclaimed, "The _____ withers, the _____ fades; but the word of our God will stand forever" (Isa 40:8).

29. When the people proclaimed King Herod god, what ate and killed him? (a) dogs; (b) a lion; (c) worms; (d) ants.

Chapter Two

〜〜〜 Jesus and His Disciples 〜〜〜

1. Quotation Puzzle: A Brief Biography

To find the verse, put the letters that appear in the bottom half of the puzzle into the column of boxes above them. The letters may not be listed in the exact order in which they appear in the quote. Mark off used letters at the bottom. A letter may be used only once. The black boxes represent the space between words.

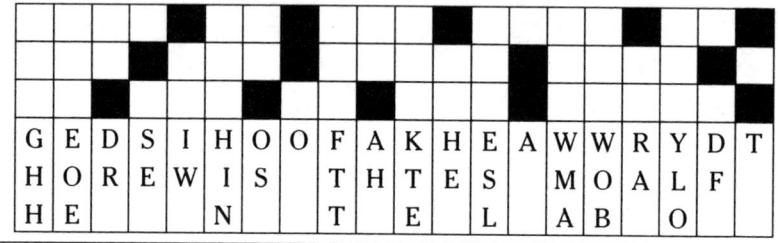

2. Who was Jesus' earthly father?

3. Fill in the blanks: Jesus said, "Go into all the _____ and proclaim the _____ news to the whole creation" (Mark 16:15).

4. When he learned of Jesus' hometown, which apostle said, "Can anything good come out of Nazareth?" (John 1:46)
(a) Nathanael; (b) Peter; (c) Thomas; (d) Andrew.

5. Jesus was "amazed" at the faith of this Gentile: (a) Cornelius; (b) a Roman centurion; (c) Luke; (d) Quirinius.

6. HIDDEN WORDS: THE BOY JESUS

These words appear in Luke 2:41–52. Find them hidden in the sentences below.

temple	teacher	parent	search	mother
festival	Passover	father	heart	wisdom

1. It takes many light years for a ray of sun to reach earth.

2. Grandma ordered tea, cherry pie, and ice cream for dessert.

3. The bus driver complained that his ear, cheek, and chin were sunburned on his left side.

4. I was asked to take part in an ecumenical songfest. I valued the experience.

5. When you look through the prize catalog, I'm sure you'll find an item pleasing to your taste.

6. I agree; kiwis do make a colorful garnish for salads.

7. Karen bought a new cage for her pet marmot. Her old one fell apart.

8. If you wish to lose a few pounds of fat, here are some exercises you can try.

9. The hunter left his compass over there under the tree.

10. We'll pick up a rental car at the airport.

7. MATCHING

Match Jesus' statement to the person, group, or occasion.

1. "Do you love me?"   A. The apostles in a storm

2. "Woe to you!"   B. Peter

3. "Be silent!"   C. Pharisees

4. "Where is your faith?"   D. Satan

5. "Away with you!"   E. Unclean spirit

8. MATCHING

Match what Jesus said to someone he healed or to that person's family member.

1. "Come out!"	A. Paralyzed man
2. "Go in peace."	B. Lazarus
3. "Get up!"	C. Gadarenes demoniac
4. "Your sins are forgiven."	D. Father of boy with demon
5. "Go home."	E. Widow of Nain
6. "Do not weep."	F. Bleeding woman
7. "If you are able!"	G. Jairus's daughter

9. This elderly prophetess, the daughter of Phanuel, spoke about Jesus in the temple: (a) Anna; (b) Miriam; (c) Deborah; (d) Huldah.

10. True or False: During Jesus' transfiguration, Abraham and Moses appeared with Jesus on a high mountain.

11. True or False: Satan told Jesus to throw himself off the Mount of Olives to prove he was God's Son.

12. CRISSCROSS PUZZLE: WORDS ABOUT JESUS

ANSWERS ON PAGE 73.

Fit each of the following 65 words into the puzzle on page 17. Words are arranged below alphabetically according to the number of letters.

4 letters	4 letters	4 letters	4 letters
acme	earn	love	seed
Amen	*Eloi*	made	sent
dear	head	name	sits
defy	hear	only	vine
doer	Lamb	Rose [of	Word
door		Sharon]	

CRISSCROSS PUZZLE: WORDS ABOUT JESUS *CONTINUED*

5 letters
above
adore
adorn
bread
enter
gives
ideal
image
mercy
might
rabbi
right

5 letters
ruler
truth

6 letters
Adonai
answer
Christ
evince
healer
living
manger
master
ransom
Savior

7 letters
believe
beloved
eternal
highest
hosanna
Messiah
radiant

8 letters
elevated
marriage
Nazareth
paradise

8 letters
Redeemer
shepherd
sonlight
strength

9 letters
ascension
beatitude
crucified
firstborn

10 letters
revelation

---

13. MATCHING

Match Aramaic phrases spoken by Jesus with their meanings.

1. *Talitha cum*   A. "Father [Daddy]."

2. *Eli*   B. "Why have you forsaken me?"

3. *Abba*   C. "Be opened!"

4. *Ephphatha*   D. "My God."

5. *Lema sabachthani*   E. "Little girl, get up."

---

14. True or False: Jesus was a descendant of King David.

15. What person was beheaded, which caused Jesus to grieve?

16. Fill in the blanks: After chasing out the money changers, Jesus told the Jews, "Destroy this _____, and in ___ days I will raise it up" (John 2:19).

---

17. UNSCRAMBLE AND SOLVE: MATTHEW 9:9–13

Rearrange the letters after each number to form a word. Then rearrange the boxed letters to form the answer to the question. The answer is a play on words.

Why did Matthew, Jesus' disciple, leave his job?

It __ __ __ "__ __ __ __ __ __ __."

1. KINGLAW ☐ __ __ __ __ __ __

2. GALON __ __ __ __ ☐

3. RENNIS __ __ __ ☐ __ __

4. HOBOT __ __ __ ☐ __

5. NERNID __ ☐ __ __ __ __

6. AXT __ __ ☐

7. USHOE __ __ __ ☐ __

8. LALC __ ☐ __ __

9. NAMES __ __ ☐ __ __

---

18. QUOTATION PUZZLE: A WAY TO OBEY

T	H	U	M	W	O	T	L	E	O	S	Y	V	U	D
O	N	E	E	V	D	U	Y	T	H	H	N	G	S	
I	O	T	O		U	R	H	T	R	I	A	O	E	
Y					E	O		D				A		

19. Fill in the blank: Jesus said, "I am the _____ of life. Whoever comes to me will never be hungry" (John 6:35).

20. The name *Christ* means this: (a) God with us; (b) bread of life; (c) anointed one; (d) Mighty God.

21. What Old Testament prophet predicted that a virgin would give birth to Jesus? (a) Isaiah; (b) Jeremiah; (c) Ezekiel; (d) Micah.

22. Who appeared both to Zechariah the priest and to Mary with birth announcements?

23. CRYPTOGRAM: WAY TO GOD

ZAYBY YXEW FR TEU, "E XU FTA VXG, XCW FTA FDBFT, XCW FTA SEHA. CR RCA IRUAY FR FTA HXFTAD AQIAJF FTDRBPT UA."

24. CROSSWORD PUZZLE: PRODIGAL SON *ANSWERS ON PAGE 78.*

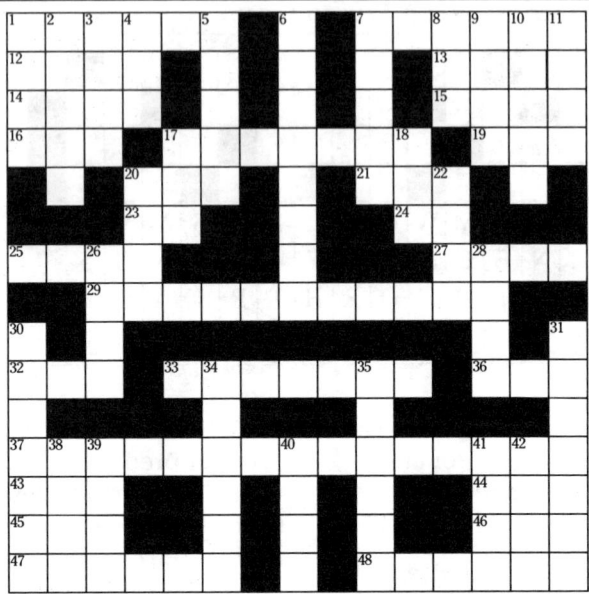

From the parable of the Prodigal Son in Luke 15:11–32

Across

1 David's son (1 Chron 3:5)

*7 Head of the family (Luke 15:12)

12 Sharpen (Ezek 21:10; present tense)

*13 "Bring out a ___" (Luke 15:22).

14 Descendant of Shuthelah (Num 26:36)

15 Son of Manasseh (2 Ki 21:18)

16 The wise __ followed the star (Matt 2:1–2)

*17 Jesus' teaching story

19 Omega (Rev 21:6)

20 Son of Jacob (Ex 1:4)

21 Son of Jacob (Ex 1:4)

23 Northwest (abbr)

24 Tellurium (symbol)

25 Large continent (Acts 16:6)

*27 Placed on son's hand (Luke 15:22)

*29 Subject of the parable in Luke 15 (2 wds)

32 Greek letter

*33 "Celebrate and __!" (Luke 15:32)

36 Used for anointing (Ex 30:25)

*37 Theme of the parable in Luke 15 (4 wds)

43 One of Noah's sons (Gen 5:32)

*44 Animal fed by 29 across

45 Son of Gad (Num 26:16)

46 "Love __ another" (John 13:34).

47 Cease employment (Num 8:25)

*48 "I have ___ against heaven" (Luke 15:21).

Down

1 One of Noah's sons (Gen 5:32)

2 Mountain of God (Ex 3:1)

3 Son of Judah (1 Chron 2:3)

4 Hebrew word for son

*5 29 across wished to eat some (Luke 15:17)

6 Agreeable (Lev 1:9)

7 Place for herds and plants (Gen 2:20)

8 ____ -la-la, singing syllable

*9 29 across returned ____ (Luke 15)

10 Fine black wood (Ezek 27:15)

11 Tear (Joel 2:13)

17 Animal foot (1 Sam 17:37)

*18 "Let us __ and celebrate" (Luke 15:23).

20 Growl

22 Emperor during Paul's day

26 _____ facto

28 To the inside of

*30 "Your ___ has come" (Luke 15:27).

31 Promised (1 Chron 29:24)

34 Monastic Jewish group

35 Social classes

38 Rabbit (Lev 11:6)

39 Eject

40 "Six days you shall do your ___" (Ex 23:12).

41 How beautiful __ the mountain (Isa 52:7)

42 Number of ungrateful lepers (Luke 17:17)

---

25. UNSCRAMBLE AND SOLVE: DORCAS (ACTS 9:36–43)

Rearrange the letters after each number to form a word. Then rearrange the boxed letters to form the answer to the question. The answer is a play on words.

How did Dorcas feel just after Peter raised her from the dead?

"__ __ __ - __ __ __"

1. KROWS ☐ __ __ __ __
2. TASC __ __ __ ☐
3. PEWNIGE __ ☐ __ __ __ __ __
4. WODWIS __ __ __ __ __ ☐
5. SHADEW ☐ __ __ __ __ __
6. TWEN __ ☐ __ __

---

26. Fill in the blanks: Jesus said, "Do not let your _____ be troubled. Believe in God, believe also in _____" (John 14:1).

27. What guided the wise men to the infant Jesus?

28. Jesus raised to life the dead daughter of this synagogue leader: (a) Jairus; (b) Zechariah; (c) Jason; (d) Nicodemus.

29. What tore in two when Jesus died?

---

30. CRYPTOGRAM: HEALED BY HIS WOUNDS

PU HZI HVFAEUE MVD VFD RDZAIXDUIIJVAI, LDFIPUE MVD
VFD JAJKFJRJUI; FWVA PJO HZI RPU WFAJIPOUAR RPZR
OZEU FI HPVNU, ZAE TQ PJI TDFJIUI HU ZDU PUZNUE.

31. UNSCRAMBLE AND MATCH: JESUS' LIFE

Unscramble the names of locations on the right, then match each event of Jesus' life with the place it occurred.

1. The Spirit of God descended on Jesus like a dove. Luke 3:21–22   _____ A. THANZEAR

2. Jesus turned water into wine. John 2:1–11   _____ B. JANDOR

3. Jesus read from a scroll in the synagogue. Luke 4:16–20   _____ C. ILEGALE

4. Jesus rode into the city on a colt. Mark 11:1–11   _____ D. THEMESANGE

5. Jesus walked on water. Mark 6:45–51   _____ E. ANAC

6. Jesus healed a centurion's servant. Matthew 8:5–13   _____ F. MEARSLUJE

7. Jesus' feet were anointed by Mary. John 12:1–8   _____ G. UNCAMPERA

8. Jesus was betrayed and arrested. Mark 14:32–50   _____ H. UMASEM

9. Jesus walked along a road with two disciples. Luke 24:13–15   _____ I. ANYTHEB

10. Jesus commissioned 11 disciples. Matthew 28:16–20   _____ J. BADSETHIA

---

32. Matching

Match the parable with the truth Jesus taught.

1. Friend at midnight   A. God's love

2. The soils (sower)   B. Persistence in prayer

3. Ten bridesmaids   C. Kingdom of God

4. Lost son   D. Beware of greed

5. The rich fool   E. Christ's second coming

---

33. True or False: Jesus wanted to share the Passover meal with his closest disciples the night before his crucifixion.

34. True or False: After John baptized Jesus, John became one of Jesus' 12 apostles.

---

35. Quotation Puzzle: The Reason for the Word

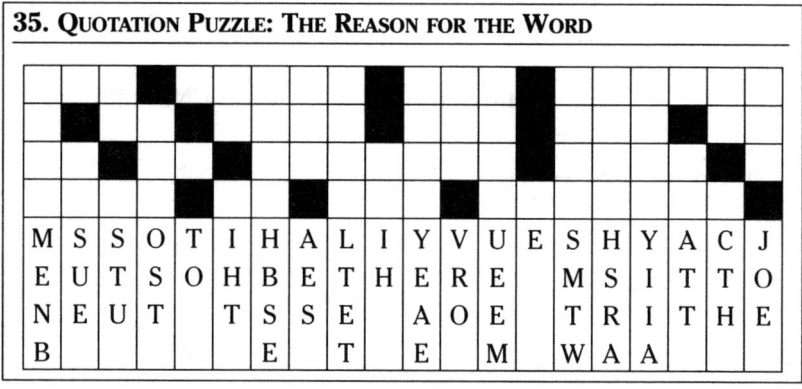

M	S	S	O	T	I	H	A	L	I	Y	V	U	E	S	H	Y	A	C	J
E	U	T	S	O	H	B	E	T	H	E	R	E		M	S	I	T	T	O
N	E	U	T		T	S	S	E		A	O	E		T	R	I	I	H	E
B						E		T		E		M		W	A	A			

CHAPTER THREE

Intriguing Places

---

1. MATCHING

Match the site of praise for Jesus with the person who praised him.

1. Praise at the cross   A. John the Baptist

2. Praise in the upper room   B. Martha

3. Praise from the womb   C. Samaritans

4. Praise at Jacob's well   D. Roman centurion

5. Praise at a tomb   E. Thomas

---

2. What was the name of the place where Adam and Eve first lived?

3. True or False: Joseph, the youngest son of Jacob, was reunited with his father and brothers in Syria.

---

4. QUOTATION PUZZLE: EVERYTHING IN ITS PLACE?

To find the verse, put the letters that appear in the bottom half of the puzzle into the column of boxes above them. The letters may not be listed in the exact order in which they appear in the quote. Mark off used letters at the bottom. A letter may be used only once. The black boxes represent the space between words.

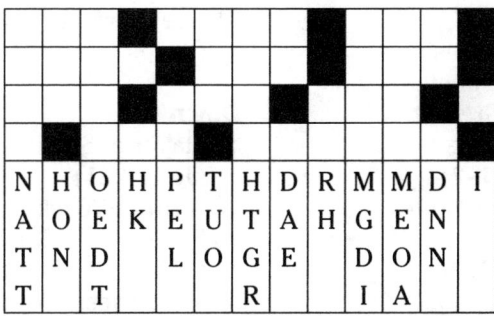

---

5. CROSSWORD PUZZLE: BIBLE PLACES *ANSWERS ON PAGE 79.*

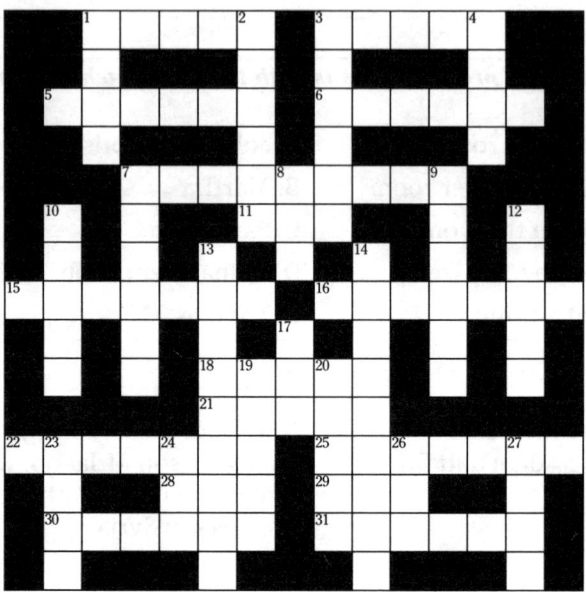

Across

1 Southern kingdom
3 Mountain in Sinai
5 Ancient Greek city (Site of Oracle)
6 A city in northern Palestine
7 Town of Jesus' birth
11 Mound of ancient ruins
15 Ancient Greek city
16 Home of Zacchaeus (Luke 19:1–2)
18 Chastizer of Job (Job 35:1)
21 Kidneys (Latin)
22 Village on Mount Olivet
25 Ancient capital on Euphrates
28 Rodent
29 Samuel's mentor
30 Save (Psa 35:17)
31 Site of watery miracle (2 wds)

Down

1 Slayer of Sisera (Judg 4:21)
2 Altitude (Ezek 17:23)
3 Father of Abdon (Judg 12:15)
4 Wilderness stopping place

7 Town in Manasseh (1 Chron 6:70)	14 David's royal city
8 Leviticus (abbr)	17 Wilderness area (Num 13:21)
9 Where Abraham took Isaac (Gen 22:2)	19 Island in the Philippines
10 Puerto Rican city	20 Husband of 1 down (Judg 4:17)
12 Brother of Abraham (Gen 11:26)	23 Work for (Hag 1:6)
13 Jesus' home on Sea of Galilee (Matt 4:13)	24 Curve
	26 Offer (Job 15:25)
	27 Son of Judah (Gen 38:4)

6. MATCHING

Match the miracle with the place.

1. Calming of the storm	A. Synagogue
2. Water into wine	B. Pool of Bethesda
3. Healing of a blind man	C. Sea of Galilee
4. Man ill for 38 years	D. Bethsaida
5. Healing of a withered hand	E. Cana

7. QUOTATION PUZZLE: THE MEETING PLACE

T	H	E	A	Y	E	N	G	M	N	H	E	T	H	E	M
W	N	E	R	E		A	M	O	T	G	I	R	T	M	R
E	H		R	R		T	W	O	E	O	R		A	D	
I	E		M	E			A	A					E	H	

8. True or False: God did not allow Moses to cross the Jordan into the Promised Land.

9. In what city did Rahab hide the Hebrew spies? (a) Jericho; (b) Zoar; (c) Bethel; (d) Shechem.

10. Fill in the blank: "I saw the holy city, the new _____, coming down out of heaven from God, prepared as a bride adorned for her husband" (Rev 21:2).

11. CRYPTOGRAM: AT THE TEMPLE

Decode the letters in the words of this Bible verse. Each letter corresponds to a different letter in the alphabet.

TBZXF ZJFXX KTVU ZJXV BEGIK JCY CI ZJX ZXYQDX, UCZ-ZCIW TYEIW ZJX ZXTAJXFU, DCUZXICIW ZE ZJXY TIK TUS-CIW ZJXY NGXUZCEIU. TIK TDD RJE JXTFK JCY RXFX TYTLXK TZ JCU GIKXFUZTIKCIW TIK JCU TIURXFU.

12. UNSCRAMBLE AND SOLVE: SEA OF GALILEE

Rearrange the letters after each number to form a word. Then rearrange the boxed letters to form the answer to the question. The answer is a play on words.

What did Peter experience at the Sea of Galilee when he tried to walk on water?

A " __ __ __ __ __ __ __ __   __ __ __ __ __ __ __ __ "

1. DWIN __ __ ☐ __

2. RINNGOM __ __ __ ☐ ☐ __ __

3. KOPES __ __ __ ☐ ☐

4. RICED __ __ ☐ __ __

5. KLINGAW __ __ ☐ __ __ __ ☐

6. HAFTI ☐ __ __ __ __

7. ONS __ __ ☐

8. VASE ☐ __ __ ☐

9. DOG ☐ __ __

10. DIES __ ☐ __ __

13. True or False: Saul was on the road to Damascus to persecute Christians when he encountered Jesus.

14. Where was Jacob's son, Joseph, taken when he was sold as a slave by his jealous brothers?

15. True or False: John was on the island of Patmos when he received his vision of the end times.

16. HIDDEN WORDS: BIBLE PLACES

Find the names of these cities and towns hidden in the sentences below:

Bethany	Tarsus	Corinth	Rome	Galilee
Tyre	Emmaus	Cana	Nineveh	Babylon

1. Jean had her last baby long ago.

2. While visiting in Portugal, I leered at the strange man.

3. With our new program, we hope to eliminate pettiness and rancor in the group.

4. Singing and playing the guitar sustains me during my lonely times.

5. The road ran from east to west across the island.

6. Meeting again at the party revived their friendship.

7. We all laughed when Emma used her hairpin to repair her typewriter.

8. "That woman can act," admitted the drama critic.

9. Nine vehicles were in the convoy.

10. Don't give Elizabeth any more bananas; she's beginning to act like a monkey.

17. MATCHING

Match the city with its nation.

1. Rameses   A. Greece

2. Damascus   B. Assyria

3. Jerusalem   C. Syria

4. Corinth   D. Egypt

5. Nineveh   E. Israel

18. QUOTATION PUZZLE: DEATH SITE

E	C	P	F	I	E	E	S	J	U	L	T	S	T	H	T	C	R	E	R
E	H	I	T	A	T	D	E	K	H	A	U	M	I	T	E	E	A	C	L
U	D	F	I	H	C	H		T	E	C			E	S	H	E		L	H
W			N		E			Y		S	A					O		T	

19. Where did Jacob dream of a stairway to heaven while he traveled to Haran? (a) Sharon; (b) Shiloh; (c) Bethel; (d) Hebron.

20. From what country was Hagar, Sarah's maid?

21. CRYPTOGRAM: HOUSE OF PRAYER

Decode the letters in the words of this Bible verse. Each letter corresponds to a different letter in the alphabet.

NJ NS QYS LINSSWQ, "PV DYTJW JDGFF HW AGFFWB G DYTJW YX ZIGVWI XYI GFF QGSNYQJ"? HTS VYT DGKW PGBW NS G BWQ YX IYHHWIJ.

22. CRISSCROSS PUZZLE: FINDING PLACES *ANSWERS ON PAGE 74.*

Fit each of the following 70 words into the puzzle below. Words are arranged alphabetically according to the number of letters.

4 letters	4 letters	5 letters	5 letters
Amam	Ijon	Hobah	Sodom
Ammi	Moab	Horeb	Syria
Arad	Nain	Lasha	**6 letters**
Aven	Road	Malta	Appius
Beer	Rome	Marah	Ararat
Cana	Secu	Media	Ashdod
East	**5 letters**	Ophel	Cabbon
Eden	Aphek	Punon	Canaan
Gath	Betah	Ramah	Dothan
Gaza	Eglon	Sidon	Garden
Home	Endor		Hebron

CRISSCROSS PUZZLE: FINDING PLACES *CONTINUED*

6 letters	7 letters	8 letters	10 letters
Ithnan	Antioch	Berothai	Alexandria
Jordan	Assyria	Damascus	Appollonia
Kartan	Corinth	Neapolis	11 letters
Lystra	Ephesus	Thyatira	Trachonitis
Rabbah	Galilee	9 letters	12 letters
Sardis	Lachish	Areopagus	Thessalonica
Shinar	Samaria	Beersheba	
Thebes	8 letters	Jerusalem	
	Arubboth	Synagogue	
	Ashkelon		

---

23. MATCHING

Match the town with one of the 12 tribes of Israel.

1. Bethlehem   A. Ephraim

2. Bethel   B. Dan

3. Joppa   C. Manasseh

4. Shechem   D. Benjamin

5. Jerusalem   E. Judah

24. UNSCRAMBLE AND MATCH: HOMETOWN

Unscramble the names of the people on the left, and match them with their hometown.

1. SEUSJ	_ _ _ _ _	A. Ur
2. THEZALIBE	_ _ _ _ _ _ _ _ _	B. Arimathea
3. HAMBARA	_ _ _ _ _ _ _	C. Nazareth
4. HESOPJ	_ _ _ _ _ _	D. Jerusalem
5. HABEERK	_ _ _ _ _ _ _	E. Jericho
6. HAISIA	_ _ _ _ _ _	F. Ain Karim (hill country of Judea)
7. CHAZSUCEA	_ _ _ _ _ _ _ _ _	G. Tarsus
8. SCRIPIALL	_ _ _ _ _ _ _ _ _	H. Uz
9. LUAS	_ _ _ _	I. Haran
10. BOJ	_ _ _	J. Rome

25. MATCHING

Match these places of war with the warriors who fought there.

1. Mount Tabor	A. Joshua
2. Hill of Moreh	B. Gideon
3. Valley of Elah	C. Barak
4. Lehi	D. Samson
5. Jericho	E. David

26. MATCHING

Match the pagan god to the place it was worshiped.

1. Marduk	A. Rome
2. Dagon	B. Canaan
3. Baal	C. Philistia
4. Jupiter	D. Ephesus
5. Artemis	E. Babylon

27. Ruth was originally from what country? (a) Moab; (b) Midian; (c) Edom; (d) Ammon.

28. On which mountain did Moses receive the Ten Commandments from God?

29. QUOTATION PUZZLE: GOD OWNS IT ALL

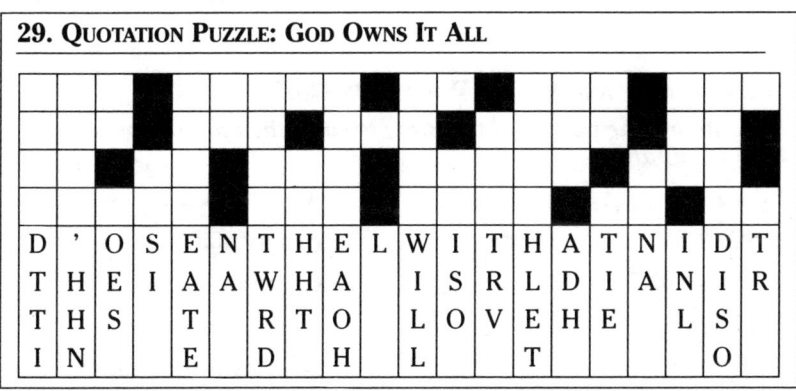

D	'	O	S	E	N	T	H	E	L	W	I	T	H	A	T	N	I	D	T
T	H	E	I	A	A	W	H	A		I	S	R	L	D	I	A	N	I	R
T	H	S		T		R	T	O		L	O	V	E	H	E		L	S	
I	N			E		D		H		L		T						O	

CHAPTER FOUR

ᗯᗯᗯᗯᗯ Heroes and Villains ᗯᗯᗯᗯᗯ

---

1. MATCHING

Match the godless son with his godly father.

1. Phinehas	A. Samuel
2. Manasseh	B. Josiah
3. Joel	C. Eli
4. Zedekiah	D. Hezekiah
5. Abimelech	E. David
6. Amnon	F. Gideon

---

2. Who was thrown into a lion's den but was not harmed?

3. This shepherd saw the burning bush: (a) Ezra; (b) Moses; (c) Joseph; (d) Benjamin.

---

4. UNSCRAMBLE AND MATCH: WHAT'S MY LINE?

Unscramble the names of the Bible heroes, then match them to their occupation.

1. RAZE	_____	A. Carpenter
2. SOMES	_____	B. Tentmaker
3. HAMEHINE	_____	C. Priest
4. TEMWHAT	_____	D. Building supervisor
5. HOPEJS	_____	E. Army commander
6. ANNAMA	_____	F. Tax collector
7. WANDER	_____	G. Physican
8. LUPA	_____	H. Fisherman
9. KLUE	_____	I. Shepherd

---

5. HIDDEN WORDS: OLD TESTAMENT HEROES

Find these names hidden in the sentences below:

Moses	Noah	David	Isaac	Jacob
Abraham	Solomon	Adam	Joseph	

1. Jack will play his violin solo Monday.

2. My father had a midlife crisis.

3. The photographer gave Linda videotapes of her performances.

4. Be sure to fill each thermos, especially the largest one.

5. Louisa accepted the job of president of the science club.

6. The Sabra hampered the enemies of the new state of Israel.

7. The answer is no; a home for criminals will not be built in this town.

8. The city of San Jose phased out its old system of tax collection.

9. Today at the Pentagon, Maj. A. C. O'Brien received a silver star for bravery.

6. MATCHING

Match the person to the musical instrument with which he is associated.

1. David	A. Pipe
2. Asaph	B. Lyre
3. Joshua	C. Cymbals
4. Jubal	D. Trumpets

7. CRISSCROSS PUZZLE: NAMES OF WOMEN

ANSWERS ON PAGE 75.

Fit each of the following 51 words into the puzzle. Words are arranged alphabetically according to the number of letters.

4 letters	5 letters	6 letters	6 letters
Anna	Ephah	Dorcas	Martha
Lois	Hagar	Esther	Phoebe
Mary	Helah	Eunice	Prisca
Neah	Lydia	Hannah	Reumah
Puah	Naomi	Hoglah	Salome
Ruth	Orpah	Huldah	Tirzah
5 letters	Rhoda	Joanna	Zeresh
Cozbi	Sarah	Judith	Zilpah
Dinah	Tamar	Keziah	**7 letters**
Eglah	Timna	Maacah	Abigail

CRISSCROSS PUZZLE *CONTINUED*			
7 letters	**8 letters**	**8 letters**	**9 letters**
Abishag	Athaliah	Sapphira	Elizabeth
Damaris	Basemath	Shimrith	Hephzibah
Ephrath	Herodias	Tryphosa	
Haggith	Peninnah		

8. Who tried to run away from God and was swallowed by a large fish?

9. To which apostle did Jesus give the keys to the kingdom of heaven?

---

10. QUOTATION PUZZLE: HANNAH'S SONG

To find the verse, put the letters that appear in the bottom half of the puzzle into the column of boxes above them. The letters may not be listed in the exact order in which they appear in the quote. Mark off used letters at the bottom. A letter may be used only once. The black boxes represent the space between words.

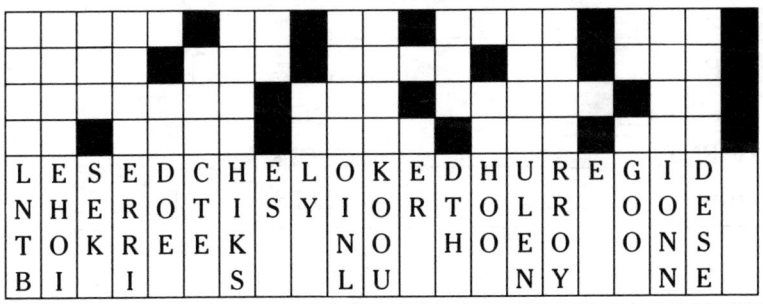

---

11. MATCHING

Match the heroic woman with her vocation or responsibility.

1. Phoebe	A. Shepherd
2. Zipporah	B. Queen
3. Candace	C. Deacon
4. Miriam	D. Merchant
5. Lydia	E. Prophet

---

12. True or False: David rejoiced over the death of King Saul.

13. True or False: It was Paul's custom to preach the gospel in the synagogue of each new city he visited.

---

14. UNSCRAMBLE AND SOLVE: SAMSON AND DELILAH

Unscramble these common words from Judges 16. Then arrange the boxed letters to find out how Samson felt after Delilah had his head shaved. The answer is a play on words.

He was "___ ___ ___ ___ - ___ ___ ___ ___ ___ ___ ___ ."

1. RAHI ___ ___ □ ___

2. ZARRO □ ___ ___ ___ ___

3. GORNST □ □ ___ ___ ___ ___

4. ORDO □ ___ ___ ___

5. WAKE ___ □ ___ ___

6. DINB ___ ___ ___ □

7. SCOLK ___ ___ ___ ___ ___ □

8. PLEES □ ___ □ ___ ___

---

15. Whom did Deborah command to defeat the army of King Jabin? (a) Barak; (b) Gideon; (c) Jephthah; (d) Sisera.

16. Fill in the blanks: "When the donkey saw the angel of the Lord, it lay down under _____; and _____ anger was kindled, and he struck the donkey with his staff" (Num 22:27).

---

17. HIDDEN WORDS: GODLY WOMEN

Find the names of eight godly women hidden in the sentences below.

Hannah	Rebekah	Elizabeth	Esther
Ruth	Sarah	Lydia	Mary

1. Nehru, the former prime minister of India, was the father of Indira Gandhi.

2. Omar, your favorite poet, was also a mathematician.

3. As she traveled west, her car continued to lose oil.

4. "Give us a rah, rah," shouted the cheerleaders.

5. There are few books in the Bible shorter than Nahum.

6. One type of loon is a grebe. Kahunas, native medicine men, collect their feathers.

7. Rick made Liz a bet her car couldn't beat his in a race.

8. Sally dialed 911 when she smelled smoke.

18. MATCHING

Match these Old Testament women with their nationality.

1. Ruth	A. Egyptian
2. Delilah	B. Sidonian
3. Haggar	C. Philistine
4. Zipporah	D. Moabite
5. Jezebel	E. Midianite

19. Fill in the blank: Paul wrote, "Only Luke is with me. Get _____ and bring him with you, for he is useful in my ministry" (2 Tim 4:11).

20. What cousin of Esther had raised her and helped her become queen of Persia and Media?

21. UNSCRAMBLE AND MATCH: WOMEN AT WORK

Unscramble the names of the Bible women on the left, then match each woman with her occupation.

1. CARDOS __ __ __ __ __ __	A. SELLER OF PURPLE
2. TERSHE __ __ __ __ __ __	B. JUDGE
3. DIALY __ __ __ __ __	C. TENTMAKER
4. HABORED __ __ __ __ __ __ __	D. SEAMSTRESS
5. ALPLISCIR __ __ __ __ __ __ __ __ __	E. QUEEN
6. NAAN __ __ __ __	F. FIELD WORKER
7. HURT __ __ __ __	G. PROPHETESS

22. QUOTATION PUZZLE: A HEALTHY SIGN

		■										■
							■					■
		■					■					■
F	H	E	U	P	A	G	M	T	L	I	E	S
T	H	O		R	I	L	H		E	O	K	E
T	L	E		R	I	S	H		T	R	U	E

23. True or False: Ishmael and Isaac, both sons of Abraham, had different mothers.

24. True or False: Delilah was Israel's only female judge.

25. Fill in the blanks: An angel told Joseph, "Do not be afraid to take _____ as your wife, for the child conceived in her is from the _____ _____" (Matt 1:20).

26. MATCHING

Match the woman with the food or drink associated with her.

1. Esther   A. Wine

2. Rebekah   B. Honey

3. Ruth   C. Milk

4. Delilah   D. Savory meal

5. Jael   E. Barley

27. CROSSWORD PUZZLE: BIBLE FACTS *ANSWERS ON PAGE 79.*

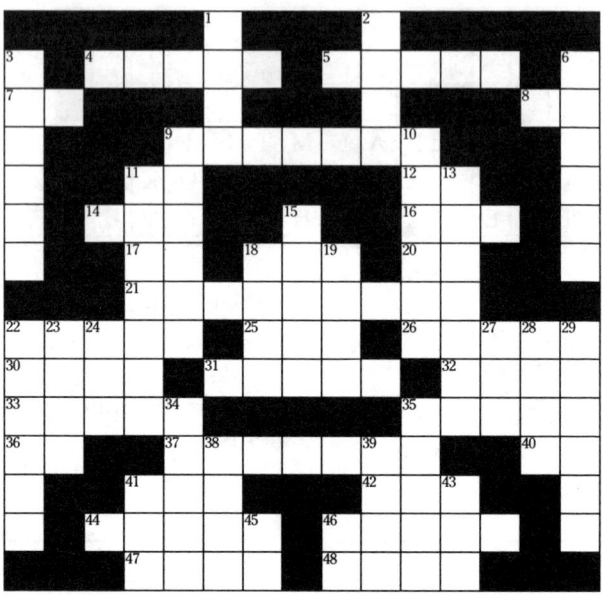

Across

4 "Let there be _____"
  (Gen 1:3).
5 Temple lights
7 Birthplace of Terah, father
  of Abraham
8 Egyptian sun god
9 Father of Isaac
11 Registered Nurse (abbr)
12 "I _ WHO I AM" (Ex 3:14).
14 Ask for charity
16 Sea in Arabia and Africa
17 Exist
18 United States of America
  (abbr)
20 Bone

21 Mother of John the
  Baptist
22 Listens
25 Ancient river near
  Ninevah
26 Women's quarters
30 Prophetess
31 Minor prophet
32 Musical passage
33 _____ ark (poss)
35 Cut sheep's wool
36 North Dakota (abbr)
37 One of David's wives
40 Right (abbr)
41 Genus of macaws
42 Book of Samuel (abbr)

44 Jewish religious festival
46 Chief of Edom
  (Gen 36:40)
47 Noah's son
48 Form of verb "to be"

Down
 1 Jezebel's husband
 2 Site of a miracle
 3 Mother of Timothy
 6 Wife of Jacob
 9 God's messengers
10 Town near Jerusalem
  (Mic 1:12)
11 Esau's mother
13 Was tossed into a furnace
  (Dan 3:19–20)
15 Rebekah's husband

18 Priest in post-exilic period
  (Neh 12:19)
19 Father (Mark 14:36)
22 Mother of Samuel
23 A slight bow (2 wds)
24 Cell component
27 Fish eggs
28 Near Jacob's tent
  (Gen 35:21 KJV)
29 Sister of Lazarus
34 Wife of Abraham
35 Bond servant
38 Foundation
39 Small island
41 First three letters of Greek
  fabulist
43 Adam was the first
45 Thulium (chem.)
46 Jewish month

28. This woman corrected Apollos's imperfect teachings about Christ: (a) Priscilla; (b) Lydia; (c) Mary of Bethany; (d) Sapphira.

29. True or False: Jacob married Rachel before marrying Leah.

30. Who came up with the plan to steal Naboth's vineyard?

31. True or False: None of the genealogies in the Scriptures list women's names.

32. Mary treasured many facts about Jesus in: (a) her mind; (b) her heart; (c) her soul; (d) her diary.

---

33. UNSCRAMBLE AND SOLVE: SNAKES ALIVE!

Rearrange the letters after each number to form a word. Then rearrange the boxed letters to form the answer to the question. The answer is a play on words.

On Mount Horeb, when Moses couldn't find enough workers to help him, how did a snake solve his problem?

It ☐ ☐ ☐ ☐ ☐ ☐ ☐ ☐ " ☐ ☐ ☐ ☐ ☐ ."

1. ALIT ☐ ☐ __ __   5. MORF ☐ __ __ ☐

2. SHUB ☐ __ ☐ __   6. DENS __ ☐ __ __

3. ALOCK ☐ __ __ ☐ __   7. NAHD __ ☐ __ __

4. FADE __ ☐ __ ☐

---

34. True or False: There were three women in Noah's ark.

35. Which of these women was not an ancestor of Jesus?
(a) Tamar; (b) Bathsheba;
(c) Rahab; (d) Abigail.

36. "Grandmother of the Year" is an award that definitely would not go to this woman:
(a) Naomi; (b) Lois; (c) Hagar;
(d) Athaliah.

---

37. MATCHING

Match the person with the sign of mourning for which he is noted.

1. Jacob   A. Wept

2. Job   B. Wore sackcloth

3. Jesus   C. Shaved head; tore robe

4. David   D. Fasted; lay on the ground

---

46 ● BIBLE QUIZZES & PUZZLES

CHAPTER FIVE

Famous Families

---

1. MATCHING

Match these Old Testament mothers and sons.

1. Eve	A. Moses
2. Leah	B. Solomon
3. Rebekah	C. Seth
4. Jochebed	D. Judah
5. Bathsheba	E. Esau

2. Who was the first child to be born of a woman?

3. True or False: During Bible times, children were seen as a blessing from God.

4. Who had seven sons and three daughters twice?

5. True or False: Lot was the father of two of his grand-children.

---

6. QUOTATION PUZZLE: A SMALL REMINDER

To find the verse, put the letters that appear in the bottom half of the puzzle into the column of boxes above them. The letters may not be listed in the exact order in which they appear in the quote. Mark off used letters at the bottom. A letter may be used only once. The black boxes represent the space between words.

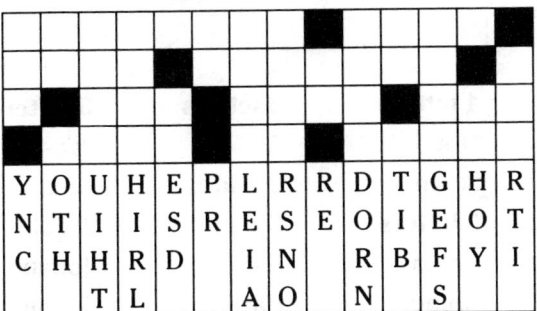

FAMOUS FAMILIES

7. CRISSCROSS PUZZLE: CHILDREN *ANSWERS ON PAGE 76.*

Fit each of the 60 words on pages 48–49 into the puzzle below. Words are arranged below alphabetically according to the number of letters.

4 letters	4 letters	5 letters	5 letters
Cain	Obed	Asher	Jacob
Elah	Shem	David	Jesus
John	**5 letters**	Dinah	Joash
Leah	Abida	Elihu	Jonah
Levi	Abihu	Haran	Judah
Nain	Ammon	Isaac	Moses

CRISSCROSS PUZZLE: CHILDREN *continued*			
5 letters	**6 letters**	**7 letters**	**8 letters**
Nadab	Jairus	Absalom	Hasadiah
Pekah	Joseph	Eliphaz	Issachar
Perez	Josiah	Ephraim	Manasseh
Sheth	Lo-Ammi	Gershom	Naphtali
Shuah	Miriam	Ishmael	Sharezer
Tamar	Reuben	Japheth	**9 letters**
Terah	Rimmon	Zebulun	Lo-ruhamah
Zabdi	Salome	**8 letters**	**11 letters**
Zerah	Samson	Adonijah	Adrammelech
	Samuel	Benjamin	**12 letters**
	Shelah		Mephibosheth

8. MATCHING

Match these married couples.

1. David   A. Keturah
2. Abraham   B. Ruth
3. Lamech   C. Drusilla
4. Mahlon   D. Ahinoam
5. Felix   E. Adah

9. QUOTATION PUZZLE: A GOOD GIFT

F	I	S	H	B	U	F	T	O	M	W	R	U	O	M	L	T	A	D	E
H	T	U	I	E	R	A	R	D	D	P	T	H	L	E	N	O	R	R	I
N	O	N	S	E		I	N	E			F	A	E	T	H	P	A	W	E
	E			S		T		A			E	R	D				R		

10. Who helped Jacob trick his father into giving him the family blessing? (a) his wife; (b) his sister; (c) his mother; (d) his brother.

11. What was Sarah's response to the news that she would bear a child in her old age? (a) she fell down and worshiped God; (b) she laughed; (c) she prayed; (d) she fainted.

---

12. MATCHING

Match these daughters with their mothers.

1. Athaliah   A. Athaliah

2. Lo-ruhamah   B. Jezebel

3. Dinah   C. Maacah

4. Jehosheba   D. Gomer

5. Tamar   E. Leah

13. MATCHING

Match these daughters with their fathers.

1. Leah	A. Saul
2. Merab	B. Hosea
3. Tamar	C. Ethbaal
4. Lo-ruhamah	D. Laban
5. Jezebel	E. Absalom

14. UNSCRAMBLE AND MATCH: MOTHER AND CHILD

Unscramble the names of these Bible children and match them with their mothers.

1. BODE	_ _ _ _	A. EUNICE
2. MAULES	_ _ _ _ _ _	B. MARY
3. MOYTITH	_ _ _ _ _ _ _	C. RUTH
4. CASIA	_ _ _ _ _	D. ELIZABETH
5. USJES	_ _ _ _ _	E. HAGAR
6. CABOJ	_ _ _ _ _	F. SARAH
7. HETS	_ _ _ _	G. EVE
8. HONJ	_ _ _ _	H. REBEKAH
9. ESHPOJ	_ _ _ _ _ _	I. HANNAH
10. LAMISHE	_ _ _ _ _ _ _	J. RACHEL

15. MATCHING

Match these sisters.

1. Oholah	A. Tirzah
2. Mary	B. Merab
3. Leah	C. Martha
4. Mahlah	D. Oholibah
5. Michal	E. Rachel

16. Who was the oldest son of Abraham?

17. What baby leaped for joy in Elizabeth's womb in the presence of Mary?

18. Fill in the blanks: "Her children rise up and call her _____; her husband too, and he praises her" (Prov 31:28).

19. QUOTATION PUZZLE: A PARENT'S PURPOSE

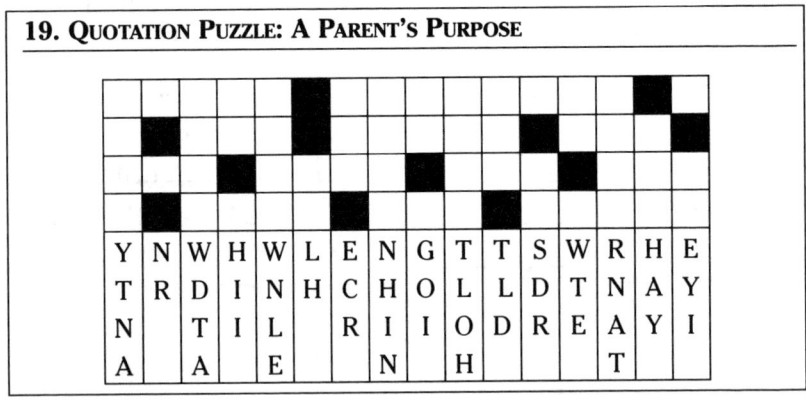

---

20. CRYPTOGRAM: CAPABLE WIFE

Decode the letters in the words of this Bible verse. Each letter corresponds to a different letter in the alphabet.

Z BZOZAKD VHED VGN BZM EHMC? RGD HR EZQ LNQD OQDBHNTR SGZM IDVDKR. SGD GDZQS NE GDQ GTRAZMC SQTRS HM GDQ.

---

21. Fill in the blanks: "As a father has compassion for his _____, so the Lord has compassion for those who _____ him" (Psa 103:13).

22. True or False: Jacob favored his oldest son, Reuben.

23. Noah cursed this grandson: (a) Gomer; (b) Canaan; (c) Cush; (d) Aram.

---

24. MATCHING

Match these grandparents with their grandchildren.

1. Eve	A. Rehoboam
2. Jesse	B. Dinah
3. Sarah	C. Obed
4. Rebekah	D. Enosh
5. Jethro	E. Esau
6. Bathsheba	F. Tamar
7. Naomi	G. Gershom

---

25. CROSSWORD PUZZLE: BIBLE COUPLES *ANSWERS ON PAGE 80.*

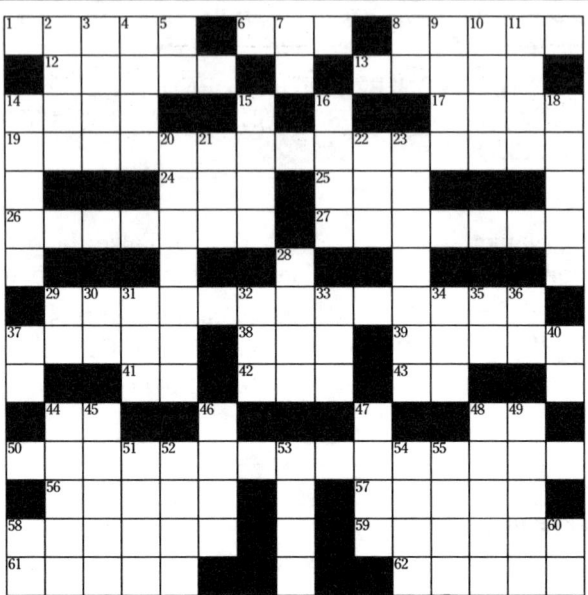

Across

1 "____ be with you" (John 20:19).

6 The Creator

8 Sister of Absalom (2 Sam 13:1)

12 Comes closer

13 Grandson of Asher (Gen 46:17)

14 Jesus was ____ in Bethlehem. (Matt 2:1)

17 Insects in lion's carcass (Judg 14:8)

19 Bible couple: Parents of Jacob (3 wds)

24 Grassland

25 First woman

26 Violent storm (Psa 55:8)

27 Coins representing a day's wage (Matt 18:28)

29 Bible couple: Parents of Jesus (3 wds)

37 Rebekah's brother (Gen 24:29)

38 Expression of greeting

39 People of Media (Dan 6:12)

41 Bible Section (abbr)

42 "Angels of God ____ him" (Gen 32:1).

43 "God saw that ____ was good" (Gen 1:18).

44 Jewish month

48 Exclamation of joy (Gen 27:27)

50 Bible couple: Parents of Isaac (3 wds)
56 One who helps
57 Home of Saul's medium (1 Sam 28:7)
58 Nightfall (2 wds) (Josh 2:5)
59 Army commander (2 Ki 5:1)
61 Topic (Psa 45:1)
62 Timothy's _____mother— Lois (2 Tim 1:5)

Down

2 Ancestor of Christ (Luke 3:38)
3 Noteworthy period of time (archaic var.)
4 Site of a wedding (John 2:1)
5 Son of Judah (Gen 38:3)
7 Amorite king (Num 21:33)
8 Tellurium (chem)
9 French clergy
10 They'll inherit the earth (Matt 5:5)
11 Space (Deut 23:12)
14 Jesus "saw a man blind from _____" (John 9:1).
15 "Strain out a _____" (Matt 23:24).
16 Produced offspring (Gen 30:38)
18 Arab clan leader
20 Philippian friend of Paul (Phil 4:3)

21 First 3 letters of famous fabulist
22 First wife
23 Son of Lot (Gen 19:38)
28 Swell of water (Jas 1:6)
29 Joint account (abbr)
30 Obadiah (abbr)
31 Spanish for "saint"
32 Noah's son (Gen 5:32)
33 Fisherman's equipment (Matt 4:18)
34 Of age (abbr)
35 Road (abbr)
36 "Oh ____ of little faith" (Matt 8:26, KJV).
37 Behold! (Isa 17:14)
40 Egyptian king (2 Ki 17:4)
44 Hebrew measure (Isa 5:10; 2 wds)
45 Newly married woman (Jer 2:32)
46 Dog's sound (Isa 56:10)
47 First human home (Gen 2:15)
48 Fragrance (2 Cor 2:15)
49 Home of Rachel and Jacob (Gen 28:10)
51 Husband of 22 down
52 "____are my mother and my brothers"(Mark 3:34).
53 Vipers (Isa 11:8; pl.)
54 Catch
55 Jewish month (Ezra 6:15)
58 "____ last" (Gen 2:23).
60 Neodymium (abbr)

26. QUOTATION PUZZLE: A SIGN OF FAVOR

H	H	E	D	T	O	G	B		F	R	O	I	T	T	O	D
S	E	R	S	W	T	M	E		A	N	D	E	W	A	H	F
T	O	R	I		A	H	E		I	R	R	E	E	D	R	A
L	O	N			A	R	E		F		U	M				E

27. Fill in the blank: "By faith _____ was hidden by his parents for three months after his birth" (Heb 11:23).

28. True or False: Timothy was the son of a Jewish mother and a Greek father, and he became a dedicated follower of Christ.

29. True or False: The children of Joseph became two of the 12 tribes of Israel.

30. Fill in the blanks: "I will pour out my Spirit upon all flesh, and your sons and your daughters shall _____, and your young men shall see _____" (Acts 2:17).

31. MATCHING

Match these women who struggled with being barren with their firstborn children.

1. Hannah

2. Sarah

3. Elizabeth

4. Rachel

5. Rebekah

A. Isaac

B. John

C. Joseph

D. Esau

E. Samuel

32. What made it difficult for Sarah and Abraham to believe God's promise that they'd have a child? (a) God's previous broken promises; (b) their age; (c) their health; (d) their belief in pagan gods.

33. What was the name of the Moabite woman who became the great grandmother of King David?

---

34. MATCHING

The birthright went to the first son. Match the father with his eldest son.

1. Abraham   A. Esau

2. Isaac   B. Amnon

3. Jacob   C. Ishmael

4. Joseph   D. Reuben

5. David   E. Manasseh

〰〰〰〰 **Extraordinary Events** 〰〰〰〰

1. At Creation, what did God name the darkness?

2. True or False: The tower that people made upon a plain in the land of Shinar to reach heaven was called Babel because God confused their language.

3. After the great Flood, what sign did God promise Noah that would indicate his covenant with every living creature? (a) thunder and lightning; (b) a dove; (c) a rainbow; (d) the bloom of a lily.

---

4. MATCHING

Match the person who died with the one who raised that person from the dead.

1. Dorcas	A. Jesus
2. Shunammite woman's son	B. Elijah
3. Jairus's daughter	C. Paul
4. Zarephath's widow's son	D. Elisha
5. Eutychus	E. Peter

5. CRISSCROSS PUZZLE: EVENTS *ANSWERS ON PAGE 77.*

Fit each of the following 53 words into the puzzle below. Words are arranged below alphabetically according to the number of letters.

4 letters	5 letters	5 letters	6 letters	8 letters
Fall (the)	anger	tithe	sorrow	prophets
fate	atone	tower	temple	resettle
foes	Exile (the)	trial	**7 letters**	**9 letters**
gate	feast	tribe	Genesis	authority
land	Flood (the)	**6 letters**	opposed	incarnate
lend	gifts	altars	silence	testament
life	light	church	slavery	**10 letters**
name	night	famine	tracing	Tabernacle
save	omers	nation	waiting	**11 letters**
sent	renew	number	**8 letters**	Crucifixion
sins	Roman	prayer	Creation	
star	sleep	priest	offering	
	spies			

6. QUOTATION PUZZLE: QUICK AS A FLASH

To find the verse, put the letters that appear in the bottom half of the puzzle into the column of boxes above them. The letters may not be listed in the exact order in which they appear in the quote. Mark off used letters at the bottom. A letter may be used only once. The black boxes represent the space between words.

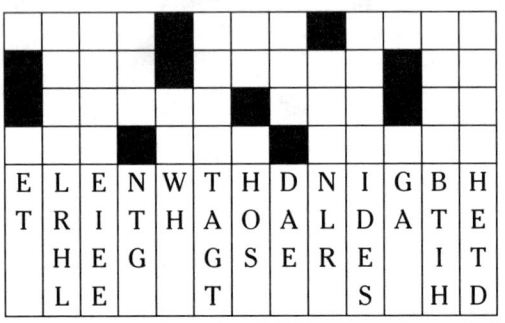

E	L	E	N	W	T	H	D	N	I	G	B	H
T	R	I	T	H	A	O	A	L	D	A	T	E
	H	E	G		G	S	E	R	E		I	T
	L	E			T				S		H	D

7. How many days and nights was Jonah in the belly of a large fish?

8. True or False: The disciples were first called Christians at Antioch.

9. Fill in the blanks: Moses and Aaron said to Pharaoh, "Thus says the Lord, the God of _____, 'Let my people _____'" (Ex 5:1).

10. Besides Eve, whom did Adam blame for his sin?

---

11. MATCHING

Match the killer with the one killed.

1. Cain		A. Goliath
2. Jael		B. Abel
3. David		C. Agag
4. Samuel		D. Eglon
5. Ehud		E. Sisera

---

12. Elijah defeated the priests of this pagan god on Mount Carmel: (a) Baal; (b) Molech; (c) Chemosh; (d) Satan.

13. Fill in the blanks: After Satan inflicted Job with loathsome sores, his wife said to him, "Do you still persist in your integrity? Curse _____, and _____" (Job 1:9).

14. True or False: God told Ezekiel to eat a scroll before speaking to Israel.

15. Fill in the blank: Then the Lord opened the mouth of the donkey, and it said to Balaam, "What have I done to you, that you have struck me these _____ times?" (Num 22:28).

---

16. CRYPTOGRAM: CREATION OF MAN

Decode the letters in the words of this Bible verse. Each letter corresponds to a different letter in the alphabet.

MJYI MJY RVWB UVB CVWSYB SZI CWVS MJY BQFM VC
MJY UWVQIB, ZIB AWYZMJYB XIMV JXF IVFMWXRF MJY
AWYZMJ VC RXCY.

---

17. HIDDEN WORDS: THE CRUCIFIXION

Within the following sentences, find the following ten people who were associated with or present at the crucifixion of Jesus:

Judas	Bandits	Simon	Barabbas	Pilate
Soldier	Priest	Centurion	Governor	Mary

1. A hungry pupil ate my lunch.

2. The "King of the Jab" Arab basked in their applause after winning his boxing match.

3. The plane was traveling over northern cities when it hit turbulence.

4. The award went to Jud, a second-year medical student.

5. Deneb and its neighboring stars make up the constellation Cygnus.

6. The Isle of Capri, established as a resort town in Roman times, is near the Bay of Naples.

7. "Sorry, you don't get a cent, Uri. Only family members are mentioned in the will."

8. When my building was sold, I erected a new one to house my growing business.

9. Once I get my diploma, Ryswick, near the Hague, is the town I'm heading for.

10. My employee gets no work done unless I monitor his every move.

---

18. UNSCRAMBLE AND SOLVE: THE GREAT FLOOD

Rearrange the letters after each number to form a word. Then rearrange the boxed letters to form the answer to the question. The answer is a play on words.

What did Noah need inside the dark ark during the storm?

" _ _ _ _ _ _ _ _ _ _ "

1. MINALAS _ _ _ _ _ ☐ _   5. LAME _ _ ☐ _

2. MELAFE ☐ _ _ _ _ _   6. NAIR _ _ ☐ _

3. TOYFR _ ☐ _ ☐ _   7. IIIIG _ _ ☐ ☐

4. DRIBS _ _ _ _ ☐   8. OVED ☐ ☐ _ _

---

19. True or False: A Jewish woman became a queen in the Persian Empire.

20. On what island did John have his vision of the end times?

21. Fill in the blanks: When Amos conveyed God's message to Israel, he stated, "Let _____ roll down like waters, and _____ like an ever-flowing stream" (Amos 5:24).

---

22. MATCHING

Match the days and Creation events.

1. Day One   A. Land animals and human life

2. Day Three   B. Light and darkness

3. Day Five   C. Rest

4. Day Six   D. Vegetation

5. Day Seven   E. Sea creatures and birds

---

23. CRYPTOGRAM: GOOD NEWS

E MA LVEZXEZX OYS XYYJ ZIQT YH XVIMU DYO HYV
MBB UFI GIYGBI: UY OYS ET LYVZ UFET JMO EZ UFI
KEUO YH JMREJ M TMREYV.

24. What happened to Uzzah when he touched the Ark of the Covenant?

25. Fill in the blanks: "For you yourselves know very well that the day of the Lord will come like a _____ in the _____" (1 Thes 5:2).

26. Who led the Israelites into the Promised Land?

27. This was *not* a plague God sent against Egypt to let His people go: (a) earthquake; (b) boils; (c) darkness; (d) hail.

28. MATCHING

Match these people to the significant events in King David's life.

1. Bathsheba   A. Prophet who confronted David about his sins

2. Nathan   B. Woman with whom he committed adultery

3. Solomon   C. Son who hung by his hair

4. Absalom   D. Son who became king

5. Samuel   E. Judge who crowned him king

29. UNSCRAMBLE AND MATCH: NOTABLE EVENTS

Unscramble the names of these Bible characters, and match the person with the event.

1. HONJA _ _ _ _ _

A. He tried to walk on water but became afraid.

2. MUSALE _ _ _ _ _ _

B. He came down from a mountain, carrying two stone tablets.

3. REPTE _ _ _ _ _

C. He was tossed from a ship during a storm at sea.

4. SEMOS _ _ _ _ _

D. He interpreted handwriting that mysteriously appeared on a wall.

5. HOJAUS _ _ _ _ _ _

E. He washed his hands to absolve himself from the guilt of crucifying Jesus.

6. MEANHIEH _ _ _ _ _ _ _ _

F. At his signal, trumpeting and shouting brought down the walls of Jericho.

7. RADIUS _ _ _ _ _ _

G. He took on the responsibility of rebuilding the walls of Jerusalem.

8. LENIAD _ _ _ _ _ _

H. He secretly anointed David king.

9. SEJUS _ _ _ _ _

I. At his command, a prophet was thrown into the lion's den.

10. LIEAPT _ _ _ _ _ _

J. A great earthquake occurred when he died on a cross.

30. CROSSWORD PUZZLE: EVERYDAY LIFE *ANSWERS ON PAGE 80.*

Across

1 "I _____ that they may have life" (John 10:10).

5 "We have seen _____ glory" (John 1:14).

8 Body of water (Luke 5:1)

12 Descendant of Ishmael (Neh 2:19)

13 Altar (Latin)

14 Medicinal African plant (Psa 45:8)

15 Second letter of Greek alphabet

16 Dashed (Luke 15:20)

17 "Prepared the Passover _____" (Mark 14:16).

18 Joseph wore a _____ _____ (Gen 37:3). (2 wds)

20 "They kept heaping many other _____ on [Jesus]" (Luke 22:65).

23 Ornate priestly vestment (Ex 25:7)

24 Objects of worship (Acts 17:16)

27 Cause of a flood (Gen 7:12)

28 Peter's protective
   garment (Acts 12:8)
29 Oven for pottery or bricks
   (Ex 9:8)
30 Armor (1 Ki 22:34)
34 Hebrew month
36 Latin prefix for "three"
37 Toward (Matt 2:8)
39 Jesus turned water to
   ___ (John 2:9).
41 Poetic evening
42 The kingdom of God has
   come _____ (Mark 1:15).
44 Father of Gaal (Judg 9:26)
45 A rule (Lev 5:10) (abbr)
46 "The Lord is the _____
   God" (Jer 10:10).

Down

1 Ancient Hebrew measure
2 "Why _____ you angry?"
   (Gen 4:6).
3 Used for sleeping
   (Mark 6:55)
4 Mountain in the Promised
   Land (Josh 8:30)
5 Gather crops (Ruth 2:21)
6 "Dies _____" (medieval
   Latin hymn)
7 Footwear (John 1:27)

8 Sacrificial animal
   (Gen 22:7)
9 Leeward side
10 Enemy of the Hebrews
   (Ezek 23:23)
11 Snakelike fish
19 Built the tabernacle
   (Ex 31:6)
20 Father of Zechariah
   (Ezra 5:1)
21 "_____ to the Lord a new
   song" (Psa 98:1).
22 Nationality of Ruth
   (Ruth 1:4)
25 Wall covering (Dan 5:5)
26 Living in temporary
   shelter (Num 24:2)
31 Plant that hid Moses
   (Ex 2:3)
32 Olive or fig (Judg 9:9, 11)
33 Portable shelter
   (Gen 9:21)
34 Wonder (Mark 4:41)
35 Baby's napkin
37 19th Greek letter
38 Metal-bearing rock
   (Job 28:2)
40 Northeast (abbr)
43 Son of Judah (Gen 38:3)

Answers and Solutions

Answers for Chapter One

1. "Who is like the wise man? And who knows the interpretation of a thing?" (Eccl 8:1).
2. True (Jonathan)
3. (d) Manasseh
4. 1D; 2A; 3E; 4C; 5B
5. See Crisscross Puzzle solution, p. 72.
6. Absalom
7. Hosea
8. False (King David and Bathsheba)
9. Goliath
10. True
11. 1. sycamore tree/Zacchaeus; 2. lion/Daniel; 3. quail/Moses; 4. olive leaf/Noah; 5. cock/Peter; 6. bees/Samson; 7. sheep/David; 8. donkey/Balaam; 9. willow tree/Jewish exiles; 10. cedar trees/Solomon
12. True
13. Josiah
14. David
15. False
16. Solomon
17. 1. sermon; 2. parable; 3. law; 4. history; 5. poetry; 6. prayer; 7. letters; 8. gospel; 9. hymn; 10. prophecy
18. See Crossword Puzzle solution, p. 78.
19. 1D; 2A; 3B; 4E; 5C
20. (c) wise men
21. Esther
22. (b) Manasseh
23. (a) I am just a child
24. "The Lord has sought out a man after his own heart; and the Lord has appointed him to be ruler over his people" (1 Sam 13:14).
25. 1. feed; 2. drink; 3. bread; 4. meat; 5. lived; 6. word; 7. eats; 8. turn; he was "raven-ous."
26. rose, lily
27. reed
28. grass, flower
29. (c) worms

Answers for Chapter Two

1. "Here is the Lamb of God who takes away the sin of the world!" (John 1:29).
2. Joseph
3. world, good
4. (a) Nathanael
5. (b) a Roman centurion
6. 1. heart; 2. teacher; 3. search; 4. festival; 5. temple; 6. wisdom; 7. mother; 8. father; 9. Passover; 10. parent
7. 1B; 2C; 3E; 4A; 5D
8. 1B; 2F; 3G; 4A; 5C; 6E; 7D
9. (a) Anna
10. False (Elijah, not Abraham)
11. False (temple)
12. See Crisscross Puzzle solution, p. 73.
13. 1E; 2D; 3A; 4C; 5B
14. True
15. John the Baptist
16. temple, three
17. 1. walking; 2. along; 3. sinner; 4. booth; 5. dinner; 6. tax; 7. house; 8. call; 9. means; ...was "taxing."
18. "In everything do to others as you would have them do to you" (Matt 7:12).
19. bread
20. (c) anointed one
21. (a) Isaiah
22. the angel Gabriel
23. Jesus said to him, "I am the way, and the truth, and the life. No one comes to the Father except through me" (John 14:6).
24. See Crossword Puzzle solution, p. 78.
25. 1. works; 2. acts; 3. weeping; 4. widows; 5. washed; 6. went; "sew-sew"
26. hearts, me
27. a star
28. (a) Jairus
29. the curtain of the temple
30. "He was wounded for our transgressions, crushed for our iniquities; upon him was the

punishment that made us whole, and by his bruises we are healed" (Isa 53:5).

31. 1. Jordan/B; 2. Cana/E;
    3. Nazareth/A; 4. Jerusalem/F;
    5. Bethsaida/J; 6. Capernaum/G;
    7. Bethany/I; 8. Gethsemane/D;
    9. Emmaus/H; 10. Galilee/C.
32. 1B; 2C; 3E; 4A; 5D
33. True
34. False
35. "But these are written so that you may come to believe that Jesus is the Messiah" (John 20:31).

Answers for Chapter Three

1. 1D; 2E; 3A; 4C; 5B
2. Eden
3. False
4. "The Lord God took the man and put him in the garden" (Gen 2:15).
5. See Crossword Puzzle solution, p. 79.
6. 1C; 2E; 3D; 4B; 5A
7. "Where two or three are gathered in my name, I am there among them" (Matt 18:20).
8. True
9. (a) Jericho
10. Jerusalem
11. "After three days they found him in the temple, sitting among the teachers, listening to them and asking them questions. And all who heard him were amazed at his understanding and his answers" (Luke 2:46–47).
12. 1. wind; 2. morning; 3. spoke; 4. cried; 5. walking; 6. faith; 7. son; 8. save; 9. God; 10. side; "sinking feeling"
13. True
14. Egypt
15. True
16. 1. Babylon; 2. Galilee; 3. Corinth; 4. Tarsus; 5. Rome; 6. Tyre; 7. Emmaus; 8. Cana; 9. Nineveh; 10. Bethany

17. 1D; 2C; 3E; 4A; 5B
18. "When they came to the place that is called The Skull, they crucified Jesus there" (Luke 23:33).
19. (c) Bethel
20. Egypt
21. "Is it not written, 'My house shall be called a house of prayer for all nations'? But you have made it a den of robbers" (Mark 11:17).
22. See Crisscross Puzzle solution, p. 74.
23. 1E; 2A; 3B; 4C; 5D
24. 1. Jesus/C; 2. Elizabeth/F; 3. Abraham/A; 4. Joseph/B; 5. Rebekah/I; 6. Isaiah/D; 7. Zacchaeus/E; 8. Priscilla/J; 9. Saul/G; 10. Job/H
25. 1C; 2B; 3E; 4D; 5A
26. 1E; 2C; 3B; 4A; 5D
27. (a) Moab
28. Sinai
29. "The earth is the Lord's and all that is in it, the world, and those who live in it" (Psa 24:1).

Answers for Chapter Four

1. 1C; 2D; 3A; 4B; 5F; 6E
2. Daniel
3. (b) Moses
4. 1. Ezra/C; 2. Moses/I; 3. Nehemiah/D; 4. Matthew/F; 5. Joseph/A; 6. Namaan/E; 7. Andrew/H; 8. Paul/B; 9. Luke/G
5. 1. Solomon; 2. Adam; 3. David; 4. Moses; 5. Isaac; 6. Abraham; 7. Noah; 8. Joseph; 9. Jacob
6. 1B; 2C; 3D; 4A
7. See Crisscross Puzzle solution, p. 75.
8. Jonah
9. Peter
10. "There is no Holy One like the Lord, no one besides you; there is no Rock like our God" (1 Sam 2:2).
11. 1C; 2A; 3B; 4E; 5D
12. False
13. True

ANSWERS AND SOLUTIONS

14. 1. *hair;* 2. *razor;* 3. *strong;* 4. *door;*
    5. *weak;* 6. *bind;* 7. *locks;* 8. *sleep;*
    ... *"dis-tressed"*
15. *(a) Barak*
16. *Balaam, Balaam's*
17. 1. *Ruth;* 2. *Mary;* 3. *Esther;* 4. *Sarah;*
    5. *Hannah;* 6. *Rebekah;* 7. *Elizabeth;*
    8. *Lydia*
18. *1D; 2C; 3A; 4E; 5B*
19. *Mark*
20. *Mordecai*
21. 1. *Dorcas/D;* 2. *Esther/E;* 3. *Lydia/A;*
    4. *Deborah/B;* 5. *Priscilla/C;*
    6. *Anna/G;* 7. *Ruth/F*
22. *"The righteous flourish like the palm
    tree" (Psa 92:12).*
23. *True*
24. *False (Deborah)*
25. *Mary, Holy Spirit*
26. *1A; 2D; 3E; 4B; 5C*
27. *See Crossword Puzzle solution, p. 79.*
28. *(a) Priscilla*
29. *False*
30. *Jezebel*
31. *False*
32. *(b) her heart*
33. 1. *tail;* 2. *bush;* 3. *cloak;* 4. *deaf;*
    5. *form;* 6. *send;* 7. *hand;* ... *became
    a "staff."*
34. *False (four)*
35. *(d) Abigail*
36. *(d) Athaliah*
37. *1B; 2C; 3A; 4D*

Answers for Chapter Five

1. *1C; 2D; 3E; 4A; 5B*
2. *Cain*
3. *True*
4. *Job*
5. *True*
6. *"Children, obey your parents in the
   Lord, for this is right" (Eph 6:1).*
7. *See Crisscross Puzzle solution, p. 76.*
8. *1D; 2A; 3E; 4B; 5C*
9. *"House and wealth are inherited
   from parents, but a prudent wife is
   from the Lord" (Prov 19:14).*

10. *(c) his mother*
11. *(b) she laughed*
12. *1B; 2D; 3E; 4A; 5C*
13. *1D; 2A; 3E; 4B; 5C*
14. 1. *Obed/C;* 2. *Samuel/I;*
    3. *Timothy/A;* 4. *Isaac/F;* 5. *Jesus/B;*
    6. *Jacob/H;* 7. *Seth/G;* 8. *John/D;*
    9. *Joseph/J;* 10. *Ishmael/E*
15. *1D; 2C; 3E; 4A; 5B*
16. *Ishmael*
17. *John the Baptist*
18. *Happy*
19. *"Train children in the right way, and
    when old, they will not stray" (Prov
    22:6).*
20. *"A capable wife who can find? She is
    far more precious than jewels. The
    heart of her husband trusts in her"
    (Prov 31:10–11).*
21. *Children, fear*
22. *False (Joseph)*
23. *(b) Canaan*
24. *1D; 2F; 3E; 4B; 5G; 6A; 7C*
25. *See Crossword Puzzle solution, p. 80.*
26. *"Sons are indeed a heritage from the
    Lord, the fruit of the womb a reward"
    (Psa 127:3).*
27. *Moses*
28. *True*
29. *True*
30. *Prophesy, visions*
31. *1E; 2A; 3B; 4C; 5D*
32. *(b) their age*
33. *Ruth*
34. *1C; 2A; 3D; 4E; 5B*

Answers for Chapter Six

1. *Night*
2. *True*
3. *(c) a rainbow*
4. *1E; 2D; 3A; 4B; 5C*
5. *See Crisscross Puzzle solution, p. 77.*
6. *"Then God said, 'Let there be light';
   and there was light" (Gen 1:3).*
7. *Three*
8. *True*
9. *Israel, go*

70 ● BIBLE QUIZZES & PUZZLES

10. *God*

11. *1B; 2E; 3A; 4C; 5D*

12. *(a) Baal*

13. *God, die*

14. *True*

15. *Three*

16. *"Then the Lord God formed man from the dust of the ground, and breathed into his nostrils the breath of life" (Gen 2:7).*

17. *1. Pilate; 2. Barabbas; 3. Governor; 4. Judas; 5. Bandits; 6. Priest; 7. Centurion; 8. Soldier; 9. Mary; 10. Simon*

18. *1. animals; 2. female; 3. forty; 4. birds; 5. male; 6. rain; 7. high; 8. dove; "flood lights"*

19. *True (Esther)*

20. *Patmos*

21. *Justice, righteousness*

22. *1B; 2D; 3E; 4A; 5C*

23. *"I am bringing you good news of great joy for all the people; to you is born this day in the city of David a savior" (Luke 2:10–11).*

24. *He died*

25. *Thief, night*

26. *Joshua*

27. *(a) earthquake*

28. *1B; 2A; 3D; 4C; 5E*

29. *1. Jonah/C; 2. Samuel/H; 3. Peter/A; 4. Moses/B; 5. Joshua/F; 6. Nehemiah/G; 7. Darius/I; 8. Daniel/D; 9. Jesus/J; 10. Pilate/E*

30. *See Crossword Puzzle solution, p. 80.*

CRISSCROSS PUZZLE: KINGS, PROPHETS, AND OTHER MEN *Puzzle on pages 6–7.*

PETER   HEZEKIAH   MOSES
PAUL   LDDER   HL   SAUL   MA
LUKE   JEREMIAH   ISAAC   CARPUS
ZZ   URIAH   EN   URIEL
TIMAEUS   DARDA
PHILIP   PILATE   AHIRAM
ONESIMUS   ZEBULUN
APOSTLE
STEPHEN   JOSEPH
THOMAS   HOSHEA   MICAH   HEGAI
ONAN   ISHBOSHETH
MELCHIZEDEK   DANIEL
NOAH   JOSIAH   JOHN
HEZRON   ANANIAS
ABIATHAR
BARIAH   AHAZIAH

CRISSCROSS PUZZLE: WORDS ABOUT JESUS *Puzzle on pages 16–17.*

```
C H R I S T           A   M A N G E R
  E   M     S       H O S A N N A     E
N A Z A R E T H       I   I   S   R   L O V E
  L   G     R   M I G H T   W O R D   A   E
R E D E E M E R       H   S   E   I   M   L       T
  R       N         E     B R E A D   G   B A D O R E
    I     G I V E S     E       G         T       U
R A D I A N T       T   M A S T E R     R I G H T
A   E   B   H   A   A   T       U       O       H
B   A   O       M E S S I A H   L I V I N G
B E L O V E D   E   C   T       E   I
I       E   E V I N C E   U       R A N S O M       F
    N       A       N   D   M     E       A         I
  S A V I O R   H     S H E P H E R D     D O E R   R
S   M       E L O I     A   R   E   B     E         S
E T E R N A L   A     O   C R U C I F I E D         T B
E       D   A D O R N   A   Y   Y   L   E           O
D O O R   O   C     O     D       I   N             R
    N     N   M   S O N L I G H T   S E N T
  E L E V A T E D   E       S       V   E A R N
    Y       I       E               H E A R
```

CRISSCROSS PUZZLE: FINDING PLACES *Puzzle on pages 32–33.*

```
A R A R A T   A P P O L L O N I A   A       I J O N
L   R     H   P         A       E ■ R A M A H   E
E D E N   E P H E S U S     G A Z A ■ A         R
X ■ O     S   E ■ A ■ H       P   D A M A S C U S
A P P I U S   K A R T A N     O                 S
N   A     A         D         L Y S T R A   M A L T A
D   G     L A C H I S H       I ■ I   O     L       S
R   U     O         S         S O D O M     T H E B E S
I   S H I N A R               O   E         M       Y
A     E   I       S       G   N             T       R
      B   C A N A A N   G A T H     B E R O T H A   I
  J O R D A N ■ M     D ■ L     A   E   A     Y ■   A
E     O       T R A C H O N I T I S E   B E T A H
N A I N       I ■ R     T   L       H O R E B     T
D ■ T     C O R I N T H     E       K   S   A M M I
O P H E L   C   A     A V E N       E   H   H     R
R   N     H         N             L     E     C A N A
    A   E           M     M O A B       P         S
S Y N A G O G U E     G A R D E N     A R U B B O T H
E     L           A       R     D         N ■ E     D
C A B B O N       S Y R I A     I         H O M E   O
U     N           T       H O B A H         N   R O A D
```

CRISSCROSS PUZZLE: NAMES OF WOMEN *Puzzle on pages 38–39.*

S	A	R	A	H			J		O	A	N	N	A				Z	E	R	E	S	H			

```
S A R A H       J   O A N N A         Z E R E S H
A     B         U             B       I     P       E
L Y D I A       D       T     A       L     H       L
O     S   A B I G A I L   S A P P H I R A   I
M     H   N   T     M     E     A     A     Z
E     A   N   H     N A O M I   H     T     A
  H O G L A H     H   A     A           P H O E B E
  A       E   A     T         R       E
E G L A H   P E N I N N A H   I         T     S
  G       H   N             S   E P H A H
  I     K E Z I A H     D O R C A S       I
  T       I   H         A     T     M
R H O D A   B         E       H A G A R
E   R     T A M A R   H U L D A H   E     I
U   P   M H       L   N   A E   R     T
M A A C A H   C O Z B I   M A R Y   R U T H
A   H   R       I   C   A O       I
H     T R Y P H O S A   E   R D I N A H   R
      H   U         I I E     Z
      A T H A L I A H   S A A       A
          H             S H E L A H
```

BIBLE QUIZZES & PUZZLES 75

CRISSCROSS PUZZLE: CHILDREN *Puzzle on pages 48–49.*

```
J E S U S   M A N A S S E H   P E K A H
A           I           P     E
C       G E R S H O M   H     R E U B E N
O B E D       I       O   E           A
B     I S A A C       S H A R E Z E R   P
      N     M         E ■ I       J O H N
T A M A R       I S H M A E L     O   T   R
  B   H         S             A   A   I
  S             H   S       I     S A L O M E
S A M U E L   M E P H I B O S H E T H   I   M
  L       O       T   U       S         O
L O R U H A M A H     A B I D A   Z E B U L U N
  M       M       H         C   E ■ E   E     H
    A     M               H A R A N   V       A
    A D O N I J A H       A ■ A   J A I R U S
J   R       S       J   T E R A H   A         A
O   A   J   S H E L A H   L       A M M O N   D
S A M S O N   E     P     I     D ■ I     A   I
E   M ■ S     R     H     P   C A I N     I   A
P E L I H U     N   E L A H   V       J O N A H
H   L ■ A       A   T     A   I
  L E A H   J U D A H     Z A B D I
    C           A
  S H E M   A B I H U
```

CRISSCROSS PUZZLE: EVENTS *Puzzle on page 59.*

```
F L O O D     O     T E S T A M E N T
A ■ F     N U M B E R     T ■ L
L I F E   I   E     I   A U T H O R I T Y
L   E   G   R     B   R ■ A ■ P       I
    R   H   S P I E S   P R O P H E T S
P R I E S T     N ■ E     S   O       H
R ■ N ■ O   T R A C I N G     S I L E N C E
A N G E R   R   A   T E M P L E   I     R
Y     R   I   R     N     D   G     U
E   R O M A N   N A M E       C H U R C H
R E N E W   L   A   S I N S   T     I
    S     T   I   A       G I F T S   L
T A B E R N A C L E   S L A V E R Y   I   L
O   T     A ■ A     E   E       X   E
W A I T I N G   N A T I O N   F   F A M I N E
E   L   A   D   O   D   O   A     O   P
R   F E A S T   N       C R E A T I O N
      E X I L E         S   E
```

ANSWERS AND SOLUTIONS

CROSSWORD PUZZLE: BIBLE DETAILS *Puzzle on pages 10–11.*

E	Z	R	A		S				T		J	O	H	N
R	E	A	P		T		Z		O		U	R	I	S
	R	H	O		O		I		R		D	E	N	
N			C	H	R	O	N	I	C	L	E			E
E	A		R		M	I	C	A	H		E		A	S
P	R	A	Y			L		M			R	A	N	T
H	E	L	P		O		A		C		R	U	T	H
E			H	O	L	Y	B	I	B	L	E			E
G	A	Z	A		D	E	B	I	R		D	Y	E	R
			J			A			A					
C	O	N	S	O	R	T		E	P	H	E	S	U	S
	T	H	E	S	C	R	I	P	T	U	R	E	S	
N		H		U		H		M						T
E	L	I	H	U		T	W	O		A	D	O	N	I
H	O	S	E	A		H		D		N	A	H	U	M

CROSSWORD PUZZLE: PRODIGAL SON *Puzzle on pages 20–21.*

S	H	O	B	A	B		P		F	A	T	H	E	R
H	O	N	E		R		L		I		R	O	B	E
E	R	A	N		E		E		E		A	M	O	N
M	E	N		P	A	R	A	B	L	E		E	N	D
	B		G	A	D		S		D	A	N		Y	
		N	W				I			T	E			
A	S	I	A				N			R	I	N	G	
		P	R	O	D	I	G	A	L	S	O	N		
B		S									T		P	
R	H	O		R	E	J	O	I	C	E		O	I	L
O				S				A					E	
T	H	E	L	O	S	T	W	A	S	F	O	U	N	D
H	A	M			E		O		T			P	I	G
E	R	I			N		R		E			O	N	E
R	E	T	I	R	E		K		S	I	N	N	E	D

78 ● BIBLE QUIZZES & PUZZLES

CROSSWORD PUZZLE: BIBLE PLACES *Puzzle on pages 26–27.*

CROSSWORD PUZZLE: BIBLE FACTS *Puzzle on pages 44–45.*

ANSWERS AND SOLUTIONS

CROSSWORD PUZZLE: BIBLE COUPLES *Puzzle on pages 54–55.*

```
P E A C E . G O D . T A M A R
. N E A R S . G . H E B E R .
B O R N . . G . B . . B E E S
I S A A C A N D R E B E K A H
R . . L E A . E V E . . . E
T E M P E S T . D E N A R I I
H . . M . . W . A . . . K
. J O S E P H A N D M A R Y .
L A B A N . A V E . M E D E S
O . N T . M E T . I T . . O
. A B . B . . E . A H .
A B R A H A M A N D S A R A H
. A I D E R . S . E N D O R .
A T D A R K . P . N A A M A N
T H E M E . S . G R A N D
```

CROSSWORD PUZZLE: EVERYDAY LIFE *Puzzle on pages 66–67.*

```
C A M E . H I S . L A K E
A R A B . A R A . A L O E
B E T A . R A N . M E A L
. S L E E V E D R O B E .
. E . A . .
. O . I N S U L T S . M
E P H O D . T . S . I D O L S
. O . D . . N . A
. L . O . P . C . G . B
R A I N . C L O A K . K I L N
. A . A . M . T
. B R E A S T P L A T E .
A B . E . T R I . E . T O
W I N E . E E N . N E A R
E B E D . R E G . T R U E
```